Our WILD™ WORLD SERIES

Whales

NORTHWORD PRESS
Minnetonka, Minnesota

© NorthWord Press, 2001

Photography © 2001: Flip Nicklin/Minden Pictures: front cover, pp. 11, 16, 37, 40; François Gohier: back cover, pp. 4, 8, 12-13, 15, 21, 33; Amos Nachoum/Danita Delimont, Agent: p. 5; Brandon D. Cole: pp. 6-7, 39; Bob Cranston/Innerspace Visions: pp. 18-19; Amos Nachoum/Innerspace Visions: p. 23; Bob Cranston: p. 24; Michael S. Nolan/Innerspace Visions: p. 26; Glenn Williams/Innerspace Visions – Ursus: pp. 28-29; Robert Pitman/Innerspace Visions: pp. 30-31; Phillip Colla/Innerspace Visions: p. 34; John K. B. Ford/Innerspace Visions – Ursus: pp. 42-43; Goram Ehlmé/Innerspace Visions: p. 44.

Illustrations by John F. McGee
Designed by Russell S. Kuepper
Edited by Barbara K. Harold

NorthWord Press
5900 Green Oak Drive
Minnetonka, MN 55343
1-800-328-3895

Library of Congress Cataloging-in-Publication Data

Corrigan, Patricia.
    Whales / Patricia Corrigan ; illustrations by John F. McGee.
        p. cm. -- (Our wild world series)
    ISBN 1-55971-780-7 (soft cover)
    1. Whales--Juvenile literature. [1. Whales.] I. McGee, John F., ill. II. Title. III. Series.

    QL737.C4 C667 2001
    599.5--dc21

                                                                    00-045569

Printed in Malaysia

10 9 8 7 6 5 4 3 2 1

Whales

Patricia Corrigan
Illustrations by John F. McGee

NORTHWORD PRESS
Minnetonka, Minnesota

IT'S NOT A FISH!

Everyone knows that about whales. But there are things we don't know about whales. Because they live in the ocean, it is difficult for humans to observe them. We don't really know for sure how many whales there are, or where they go on annual migrations. And we don't know exactly how they find their way on each journey.

Scientists who study animals are called zoologists (zoe-OL-uh-jists). Many of them spend hours and hours trying to learn more about the habits and daily lives of whales. There are still many mysteries yet to be solved.

Fin whales are sometimes called "greyhounds of the sea" because they swim very fast. They are known for making a huge spout or "blow."

Orcas may travel as far as 100 miles in a day. They prefer cool, deep water but may approach the shore to find food.

There are many species (SPEE-sees), or kinds, of whales. They have some things in common, like living their entire lives in saltwater and coming to the surface to breathe. They are all mammals and usually have one baby at a time, called a calf. They are carnivores (KAR-nuh-vorz), which means they eat meat.

Whales also have differences. Some leap up and out of the water, while others surf along the top of the waves. Some whales have teeth and some do not. Some use a kind of sonar, like bats, to navigate and find food. Whales come in many colors, from white to black. Some are small and sleek, while others are very large.

Some whales, like the bowhead, may live forty years. Others, like the sperm whale, may live over seventy years.

Many whales travel alone, and others live in family groups called pods. Some whales communicate with clicking sounds, while others make sounds that remind us of songs.

Anytime during the year, humpbacks may soar high out of the water. During the winter breeding season, they may do it to show off and help attract a mate.

Orcas are actually the largest member of the dolphin family, but they are fierce hunters. They sometimes even ride the waves toward shore while chasing food.

All whales are classified as cetaceans (see-TAY-shins). This scientific order also includes dolphins and porpoises, which are close relatives of whales.

Researchers believe there are more than seventy-seven species of whales, dolphins, and porpoises.

Cetaceans are divided into two types: those with teeth and those without teeth. Most of the smaller whales and all of the dolphins and porpoises have teeth. Some have only a few, and some have many. The narwhal, for instance, has two teeth, and the sperm whale has about fifty-five.

There are thirty whale species with teeth. They eat the same way as any toothed animal, using their teeth to catch food and to chew. Toothed whales eat fish, squid, and other sea animals.

Whales
FUNFACT:

Whales swim through the water by moving their tails up and down. Fish swim by moving their tails side to side.

To find food and navigate through the water, all toothed whales use a kind of sonar. It is a system called echolocation (ek-oh-lo-KAY-shun). As a whale travels through the dark seas, it makes clicking sounds. Those sounds bounce off objects in the water, like rocks or fish. When the sound waves return, the whale receives a vibration in its jawbone, all the way back to its internal ear. That's how toothed whales "hear" where food is. With echolocation, whales are able to tell the size of an object in the water and its exact location.

There are eleven whale species without teeth. They eat tiny fish and shrimp-like creatures called krill, which are only 2 inches (5 centimeters) long.

These whales may have up to several hundred baleen (buh-LEEN) strips in their mouth. They are long strips of hard fibers made of material similar to human fingernails. The strips grow close together and work like a filter or strainer.

When baleen whales eat, they open their mouths to take in krill, small fish, and water. Then they strain out the water through the baleen, and keep the food to swallow. Some baleen whales, like humpbacks, have long grooves, or pleats, in the skin along their throats. These grooves expand like an inflated balloon when the animals feed, and allow the whales to take in huge quantities of food and water.

All whales, including this humpback, must be able to open their mouths very wide to take in the food they need to stay healthy.

When humpbacks feed together in a group, they may all lunge toward the surface at the same time. This movement makes the water seem to "boil."

The earliest whales are said to have been land animals, mammals with four legs and hair on their bodies. About fifty million years ago, these animals returned to the sea. Over millions of years, whale bodies have changed so that these mammals could live more comfortably in water.

For instance, the nose became an opening called a blowhole located on the top of the head. Each blowhole has a valve that closes to keep out water when the whale is underwater. Toothed whales have just one blowhole. Baleen whales have two of them.

Today, most of the body hair on whales is gone, although some of them still have a few hairs on their snouts. The front legs became flippers. And as whale bodies became more streamlined for swimming, the back legs disappeared.

Whales
FUNFACT:

In general, baleen whales are larger than toothed whales. But toothed whales are thought to be more intelligent.

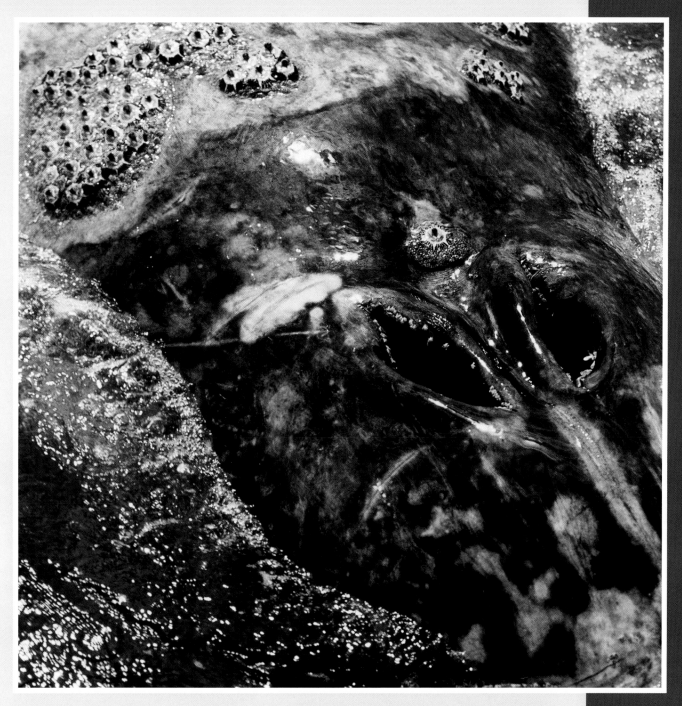

When a gray whale pokes the top of its head above
the water, it just opens its blowholes to breathe.
Whales do not breathe at all through their mouths.

Whale tails, called flukes (FLOOKS), are very strong and muscular. They developed to help the whale swim through the water.

The ears, which were once on the outside of the head, became small internal openings. The lungs grew larger to help the whale stay underwater longer when hunting for food. Whale lungs are much more efficient than human lungs.

The sperm whale tail is easy to identify. It has two wide, triangular flukes with a deep notch in the middle. It may measure over 13 feet (4 meters) from tip to tip.

Whales also developed a layer of body fat, called blubber. It helps them float and swim to the surface to breathe, especially calves. It also provides natural insulation, to help whales maintain a healthy body temperature in the ocean water.

All of these changes took place a long time ago. In fact, whales have not changed much in the past five million years. What has changed is how we think about whales.

Early reports from nervous sailors and explorers often described giant whales as vicious sea monsters. Native tribes used whales as a source of food. For nearly a hundred years, the oil from some species was used to light oil lamps and to grease machinery in factories. Baleen strips were used to make buggy whips, umbrellas, and lampshades. In a few countries, people ate whale meat. In other countries, the meat was used as food for dogs. During this time, many whale species came close to extinction (ex-TINK-shun), or being wiped out completely.

Whales
FUNFACT:

The layer of blubber on a whale may be as thick as 2 feet (61 centimeters).

This human diver taking photographs of a right whale seems tiny.

During the 1960s, people became interested in conservation (con-ser-VAY-shun), or finding ways to protect whales. They learned that whales are gentle animals. Fishermen began taking people out in their boats to see whales. Over time, many people joined the worldwide movement to save the whales.

In 1986, an agency called the International Whaling Commission declared a moratorium (more-a-TOR-ee-um), or a stop, to hunting, saying that we must protect whales. Most countries agreed, and still do not allow hunting today.

At the same time, the governments of some countries established marine sanctuaries (SANK-choo-air-ees), or safe places, for whales to feed, mate, and give birth to their young.

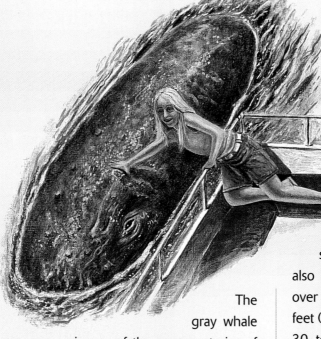

The gray whale is one of the success stories of the conservation movement. Twice in history, gray whales were nearly extinct. Today, there are about 22,000 of them living in all the world's oceans.

In fact, in the lagoons of Mexico, gray whales often approach small boats full of whale watchers. These animals have become known as *amistosa* (ah-me-STOW-suh), a Spanish word that means "friendly."

Some of the whales raise their huge gray heads up out of the water, perhaps to look at the whale watchers. This is called spyhopping. If the whales are close to the boat, they may allow the whale watchers to touch them. Only gray whales ever allow humans to touch them.

While most of the stocky body is gray, these whales also have white splotches scattered all over it. Gray whales grow to about 50 feet (15.2 meters) and weigh as much as 30 tons (27,000 kilograms). They are baleen whales. When feeding, they swim sideways along the ocean floor, scooping up small fish, krill, and bits of seaweed.

Gray whales travel in small groups of about three or four. They migrate each year from the seas of the far north all the way south to the warm lagoons off Mexico's Baja Peninsula. They swim close to shore, and can easily be seen from beaches and seaside cliffs. This 6,000-mile (9,600-kilometer) trip is one of the longest migrations of any animal on the planet.

The gray whale has about 160 pairs of short, smooth baleen plates. They are about 15 inches long and 10 inches wide. They are gray with yellowish bristles.

Humpback whales also migrate, but they are best known for their acrobatics. These black whales grow to 62 feet (19 meters) and weigh up to 53 tons (48,000 kilograms). The humpback has a small, upright fin on its back, called a dorsal fin. Some whales have large ones, some have small ones, and some have none.

The humpback's black and white flippers are 15 feet (4.5 meters) long, much longer than those of any other whale. These whales sometimes lie on their sides and repeatedly smack a flipper on the surface of the water. Scientists aren't sure why they do this. It may be to mark their territory or send a message to other whales. The sound of that powerful flipper hitting the water is very loud!

Sometimes, humpbacks slap the water with their flukes. This is called lobtailing. And it's really loud too. A humpback's powerful tail often measures up to 12 feet (3.6 meters) across.

The underside of each humpback's tail has a one-of-a-kind pattern. Like many whales, humpbacks lift their tails high out of the water before making a deep dive. This is called throwing the flukes. It is a good opportunity for researchers to see the markings and identify the individual whale. They can then track a whale on its migration and learn where it goes, year after year.

There are about 100,000 humpbacks living in oceans throughout the world.

Sometimes, humpback whales jump up and out of the water and then fall back with an enormous splash. This is called breaching. Humpbacks often breach more than once. A few other whale species also breach, but none as often as the humpback.

Humpback whales are baleen whales, and they eat krill and small fish. They often feed alone, but sometimes, they search for food with other whales. This is called cooperative feeding.

Groups of ten or twelve individuals swim in circles under-water, blowing bubbles through their blowholes. The thick net of bubbles traps the fish and krill.

The whales open their huge mouths and swim up through the bubbles, taking an easy meal. The humpback is the only whale that hunts using bubbles like this.

This humpback calf has a lot of growing to do before it catches up to the size of its mother. It sometimes rests by "hitching a ride" to the surface.

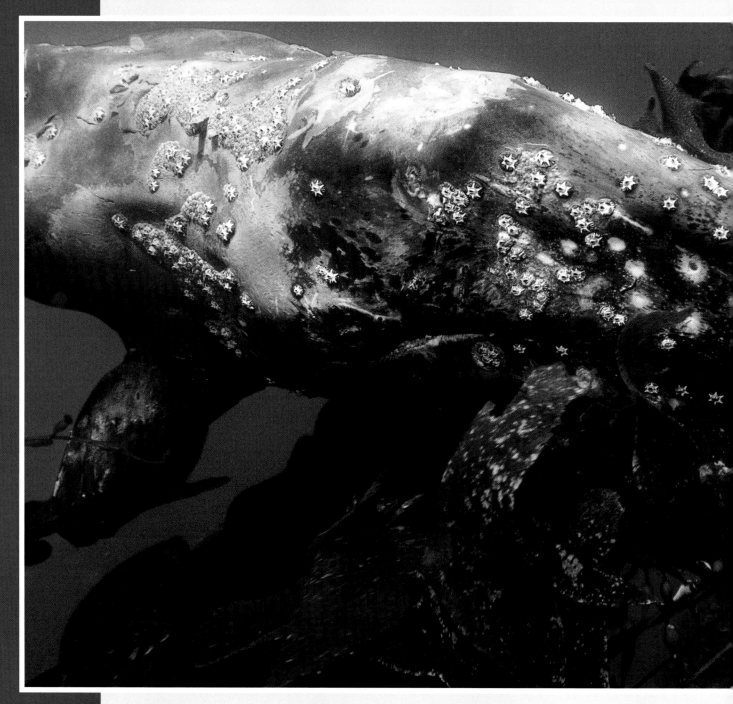

Gray whales make a variety of grunting, clicking, and whistling noises to keep in touch with others in their pod.

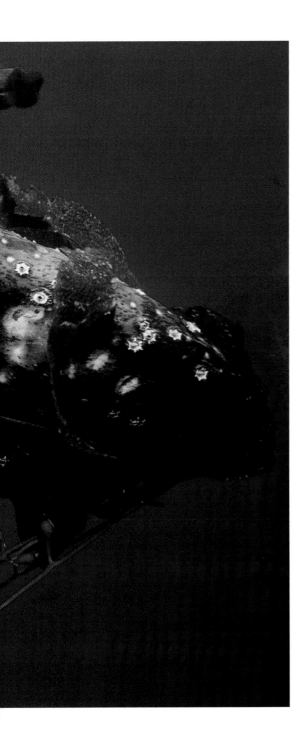

Almost all whales make vocalizations (vo-kul-ize-A-shuns), or sounds, to communicate with one another, but no whale sounds like the humpback. With their heads down low in the water and their tails high above them, these whales make sounds that go on for as long as 30 minutes or more.

These long, slow songs can be heard with the help of a hydrophone, which is a microphone that works underwater. For years, we thought that only male humpbacks sang these songs, perhaps to attract a mate. Today, we know that females also sing.

Whales
FUNFACT:

The arteries of a humpback whale are large enough for a human toddler to crawl through.

Fin whales usually appear in small groups of two to seven individuals.
They feed mainly on krill, and occasionally herring.

While humpbacks are famous for singing, the fin whale is famous for swimming fast. It is also called a finback, and sometimes "the greyhound of the sea." It has a long, narrow head and a streamlined body designed to move quickly through the water. Fin whales can swim up to 20 miles (32 kilometers) per hour!

Second in size only to blue whales, fin whales grow to 85 feet (26 meters) in length and weigh as much as 80 tons (73,000 kilograms). They have slender bodies and vary in color from dark gray to dark brown. The right side of each animal's mouth is white. As their name suggests, they have a fin on their back.

Fin whales are baleen whales, but they feed differently from humpbacks. They search for food alone, and use a method called lunge feeding. After a deep dive, the whale races up toward the surface at an angle, directly into a school of small fish. It lunges out of the water with its mouth wide open and its throat pleats full of food and water!

After a whale dives, the air in its lungs is hot and moist. A spout is made when that air is blown out the blowhole and meets the colder air outside. Fin whales have two blowholes, and they make very large spouts, or "blows." The cone-shaped fog may spray up to 20 feet (6 meters) in the air.

Unfortunately, fin whales are endangered. Only about 50,000 to 100,000 still swim throughout the oceans of the world.

If necessary, the bowhead can create its own breathing holes under the frozen sea by breaking through ice up to 12 inches thick!

The bowhead (BO-head) whale and the right whale are so similar that they were once thought to be the same species. They have no dorsal fin. Both are baleen whales (but the bowhead's baleen is twice as long as that of the right). They are both mostly black and they have very wide flukes, sometimes equal to half their body length.

Male bowheads grow to lengths of 50 feet (15 meters) and weigh as much as 65 tons (60,000 kilograms). Females are even bigger. Bowheads have a white patch on the chin. They are a protected species. Scientists estimate that there are about 8,000 bowheads left.

They live in the frigid Arctic regions, where they usually swim very slowly. Occasionally they have been sighted swimming upside down.

Whales
FUNFACT:

The longest baleen ever measured was 14 feet (4.3 meters), from a bowhead whale.

Bowhead flukes may be as wide as 27 feet (8.1 meters). And these whales have a thick layer of blubber to help keep them warm.

Right whales are about the same length as bowhead whales, but they are heavier, weighing as much as 70 tons (64,000 kilograms). The bodies of right whales are rounder than bowheads, and they have short, spade-shaped flippers. Some right whales have a white patch on their belly.

Right whales have whitish, scaly growths called callosities (kal-OSS-it-ees) on the snout that form a tough covering. The pattern of the callosities is a way to tell individuals apart.

The largest population of right whales lives off Argentina, though some right whales live in the North Atlantic Ocean. They got their name because they were considered the "right" whale to hunt, for their valuable oil. Today, right whales are endangered, with only about 4,500 of them in the northern and southern regions combined.

Whales
FUNFACT:

Whales take short naps from time to time, any time of the day or night. When right whales sleep at the surface, they sometimes snore.

Right whales often have "whale lice" living on their callosities. These tiny creatures don't hurt the whales, but instead feed on dead, shedding skin.

Mother and calf blue whales keep in touch with sounds that can travel for many miles underwater. They are probably the loudest animals alive, louder than a jet engine.

The blue whale is also in serious danger of extinction. Only about 5,000 of them still swim the world's seas.

Blue whales aren't exactly blue. They are blue-gray with mottled, or speckled, skin. They have tiny dorsal fins, only about 2 inches (5 centimeters) high, compared to the 6-foot-tall (1.8 meters) dorsal fin of the male orca.

When a blue whale begins a deep dive, its small dorsal fin rises slightly out of the water. Blue whales do not lift their flukes high out of the water as other whales do. They hold them flat, just above the surface as they begin the dive.

Blue whales are even bigger than the biggest dinosaurs. They can grow up to 90 feet (27 meters) or more.

A blue whale may weigh as much as 110 tons (100,000 kilograms), or about the same as twenty-two elephants. They are baleen whales that eat up to 2 tons (1,800 kilograms) of krill each day.

These giants of the sea have calves every two or three years, about twelve months after mating. At birth, a blue whale calf may measure 25 feet (7.5 meters) and weigh about 7 tons (6,300 kilograms). Newborn calves of other whale species are smaller.

Most whale calves nurse for up to two years. During that time, a blue whale calf drinks about 100 gallons (380 liters) of milk every day. That means it might gain more than 200 pounds (90 kilograms) in one day!

At first, calves do not have much blubber to make floating easy. So whale mothers must help them to the surface to breathe. After a short time the calves are strong enough to surface on their own. But they usually stay very close to their mothers so they can learn new things.

Whales
FUNFACT:

The heart of a blue whale is the size of a Volkswagen Beetle. Its tongue is big enough for a full-grown elephant to stand on it.

Whales have big brains and are believed to be very intelligent and able to learn easily. In fact, male sperm whales have the biggest brain of any creature on Earth, weighing up to 20 pounds (9 kilograms). Scientists, who have brains that weigh about 3 pounds (1.35 kilograms), have no idea what sperm whales think about all day!

Sperm whales are dark gray or dark brown, and they have wrinkled skin. They have a hump on their back, but no dorsal fin. Sperm whales grow to about 60 feet (18.5 meters) and weigh as much as 50 tons (45,000 kilograms). They have large heads full of rich, waxy oil called spermaceti (sperm-uh-SET-ee). That's where their name comes from.

Today, about 2 million sperm whales swim throughout the oceans of the world. Sperm whales live in deep water, and they dive deeper than any other whale—as far down as 3,300 feet (1,000 meters). They can stay underwater for as long as an hour before coming to the surface to breathe. These deep dives may be possible because the oil in the animal's head becomes solid as the whale dives. That makes it act like an anchor to take the whale deeper.

The narrow lower jaw of the sperm whale is about 15 feet (4.5 meters) long. All of its large teeth are on the lower jaw. When the sperm whale's mouth is closed, its cone-shaped teeth fit nicely into cone-shaped spaces in the upper jaw.

Each tooth may measure as long as 7 inches (18 centimeters). In the 1800s, whalers would carve drawings into teeth they collected, sometimes ships or lighthouses, sometimes other animals. This art is called scrimshaw.

Sperm whales usually eat large squid and fish. Animals hunted for food are called prey (PRAY) animals. Some scientists think the sperm whale attracts its prey by allowing its lower jaw to hang open. When light from the sun reflects off the whale's big white teeth, curious squid and fish may swim closer to investigate, and become a meal for the whale.

The sperm whale rarely shows much of its body above the water.
It has one blowhole, which is toward the left side of the head.

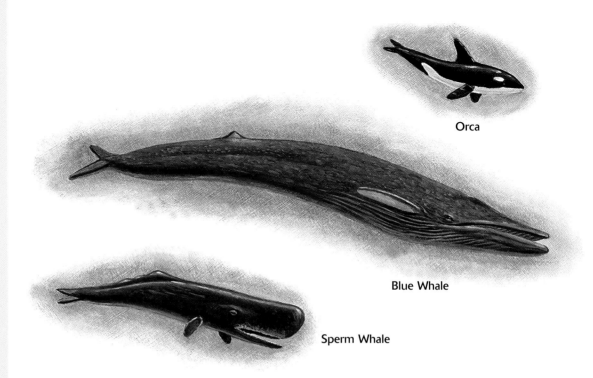

Orca

Blue Whale

Sperm Whale

Orcas also have large teeth, and are sometimes known as "killer whales" or "wolves of the sea." They can grow to about 31 feet (9.5 meters) and weigh up to 9 tons (8,200 kilograms). Orcas eat about 250 pounds (113 kilograms) of food each day.

These fearsome whales may swim long distances to find prey like fish, seals, sharks, birds, and turtles. Orcas sometimes hunt young blue whales. They also have been known to attack other baleen whales that are old or ill.

Orcas are easily identified by their black and white markings, like the white oval just behind each eye. Also, their tall dorsal fins stick high above the water when they swim at the surface. And just behind the dorsal fin is a grayish patch, sometimes called a "saddle."

The shape of the patch is unique on each animal, which helps researchers recognize individual whales. Orca calves are born pale yellow and black, and later, the yellow changes to white.

Orcas live in all the oceans of the world and are not endangered. We don't know how many there are because no one has ever tried to count them. Their pod may include up to thirty relatives. Orcas usually stay in the same pod for their whole lives. They sometimes hunt their prey together and then share the food. Pods migrate together and often take care of calves together.

Orcas make a variety of clicks and squeals as a way of staying in touch with one another. Some sounds mean there is food nearby. Some sounds are made only when a family group meets other relatives. And some are the sounds that a mother and calf use to communicate.

To see a breaching orca is every whale watcher's dream. The color markings and wide flippers are easy to identify.

Belugas are also called white whales. The average size of a beluga pod is ten members. They often spyhop to take a look around.

The beluga (beh-LOO-guh) whale is known as the "canary of the sea" because of the many unusual-sounding chirps and squeals it makes. Belugas are born grayish brown, but by the time they are six years old, they are pure white.

In the world of whales, belugas are relatively small. They have a round, plump body with no dorsal fin. They only grow up to 16 feet (5 meters) and may weigh just 2,400 pounds (1,100 kilograms). Belugas have teeth and prefer to eat fish and squid.

Belugas often gather in pod groups of hundreds of individuals for migration. Between 50,000 and 70,000 belugas live in the icy Arctic, but in spring and summer, about 600 of them travel to the Saint Lawrence Seaway in Canada.

Whales
FUNFACT:

Researchers can tell how old a whale is by counting the layers, or rings, of growth on its tooth. It is the same method used for telling the age of a tree.

Pages 42-43: Belugas are generally slow swimmers, but they can swim forward and backward. And they are often seen in very shallow water near the snow-covered shore.

The tip of the narwhal tusk is white and usually smooth.
Researchers have seen narwhals with two tusks, but it is very rare.

The narwhal also lives in the very cold waters of the Arctic, where scientists estimate the population to be about 30,000. Narwhals often live near shore in bays, and they can be seen swimming around floating ice.

We don't know much about them, but if you ever see one, you'll have no trouble identifying it! Some people know them by their nickname, "unicorn whale."

A narwhal's body only grows to be about 16 feet (5 meters) long. But the tusk of an adult male can be up to an additional 8 feet (2.5 meters) long. The tusk is actually a hollow tooth that grows in a counterclockwise spiral shape out of the left side of the whale's jaw.

Some narwhals use their tusks in battles with other males. They may use them to defend their territory and to compete for females during mating. Zoologists aren't sure if tusks have any other purposes.

These slow-swimming whales are blue-gray to brownish with lighter spots and blotches on the back. They have no dorsal fin and weigh about 3,500 pounds (1,575 kilograms). Even with only one regular tooth, they somehow eat squid, fish, shrimp, and crab. Scientists aren't sure how narwhals manage to eat such large prey.

We may never solve the many mysteries surrounding the lives of whales. That's okay. We will continue to study them, and they will continue to fascinate us as long as they spout and spyhop and swim in their ocean homes.

Internet Sites

You can find out more interesting information about whales and lots of other wildlife by visiting these web sites.

http://endangered.fws.gov	U.S. Fish and Wildlife Service
www.cetacea.org	Whale and Dolphin Conservation Society
www.discovery.com	Discovery Channel Online
www.enchantedlearning.com/subjects/whales	Zoom Whales at Disney Online
www.fmri.usf.edu/mammals.htm	Florida Marine Research Institute
www.kidsplanet.org	Defenders of Wildlife
www.nationalgeographic.com/kids	National Geographic Society
www.nwf.org	National Wildlife Federation
www.worldwildlife.org	World Wildlife Fund

Index

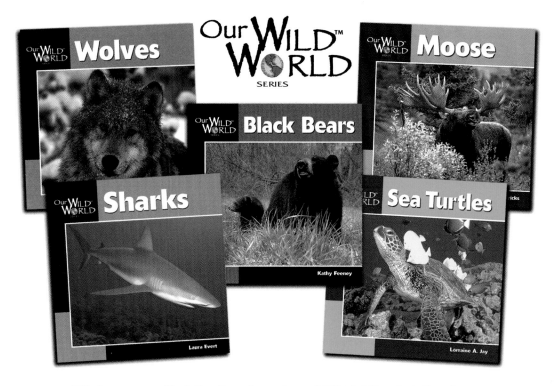

Titles available in the Our Wild World Series:

BISON
ISBN 1-55971-775-0

MANATEES
ISBN 1-55971-778-5

WHALES
ISBN 1-55971-780-7

BLACK BEARS
ISBN 1-55971-742-4

MOOSE
ISBN 1-55971-744-0

WHITETAIL DEER
ISBN 1-55971-743-2

DOLPHINS
ISBN 1-55971-776-9

SEA TURTLES
ISBN 1-55971-746-7

WOLVES
ISBN 1-55971-748-3

EAGLES
ISBN 1-55971-777-7

SHARKS
ISBN 1-55971-779-3

See your nearest bookseller or order by phone 1-800-328-3895

NORTHWORD PRESS
Minnetonka, Minnesota